Phenomena

Eduards Aivars

About the translator

Jayde Will is a literary translator working from Lithuanian, Latvian, and Estonian. His recent or forthcoming translations include Daina Tabūna's short story collection *The Secret Box* (The Emma Press), Ričardas Gavelis's novel *Memoirs of a Life Cut Short* (Vagabond Voices), Artis Ostups's poetry collection *Gestures* (Ugly Duckling Presse), and Inga Pizāne's poetry collection *Having Never Met* (A Midsummer Night's Press). He lives in Riga.

Contents

Part Three

Part One

THE POSTMAN DOESN'T KNOCK ANYMORE

A poem slides under the door
You are still standing frozen and think, if
It's an unpaid bill with interest
It's not
When you realise it's something good, you still don't open it
You're afraid, that I will ask to stay the night
I could
But that's not my intention
I just go to houses, which aren't renovated
And do what is still possible
I also don't see, what's happening on your faces

THERE'S UNREST IN MY HEAD FACTORY THIS MORNING

The night workers don't want to go home
They are tired, but they're afraid of losing their jobs
In the morning, when they open up my head's gates
The night shift workers await the day shift workers in the
    factory's courtyard
With bombs of nerves

AT YOUR FATHER'S HOUSE WHERE YOU SPENT YOUR SUMMERS

The windows on that side of the house look out to the
  jasmine bushes
On the other side there are two cedars growing
Along with the pitch-black night
But someone is chopping wood in the shed—
He wants to chop a gigantic log in two like time
The wood chips fly in my dream like moments

AND MY FATHER PASSED AWAY

There will be far less laughter
And well-aimed barbs
There won't be anyone, who will put
A whole egg in their mouth
My mother is coming over the hill
With a paper bag of sweets
And a cold sore on her lips

MAGDA THE MINESHAFT STEWARDESS

Had ice cream smeared around her mouth
Just another girl from my class
I was from Kraslava, she was born in Dagda
Nobody dared to touch Magda because of her temper
She was stronger than all the boys in the class
She headed the formations, was the best in GTO classes[1]
She grew up and became interested in the Near East
She was in Iran, later in Baghdad
It was there she already carried a child under her heart
She read her exalted poetry
She got married in Krakow unexpectedly
And now everyone goes to the salt mines
To Magda the mine shaft stewardess—
She was called that because of her fancy uniform
We heard a gut-wrenching story
About the death of the workhorses there – underground
She remembered me
However she was as cold as a stone wall
She was almost tipping over from talking so much
But with clicking heels deep below the earth
And ice cream around her mouth up on the surface

---

1 Ready for Labour and Defense of the USSR (Gotov k trudu i
oborone SSSR), one of the physical educations programmes in the
Soviet Union.

HE PARTIED WITH HIS FRIENDS UNTIL LATE IN THE NIGHT

Each slept where they were able to
In the morning he surprised his friends
With the fact that upon waking up he had a tan
In his dream he had been in the desert
'You were acting a little strange yesterday,' one of them said

AS SOON AS I OPEN THE CURTAINS

The flower pot falls from the windowsill
That happens every morning
There's something wrong with the windowsill
There's something wrong with the flower pot
There's something wrong with me
Sometimes I catch it
Other times it ends up falling
The pot is made of plastic
The plant is eternal

OH, HE CAUGHT FIRE FROM THE CITY'S LIGHT

And while humming he went back
Failing to understand, that he was burning
He entered his home village like a torch

No one from the village
Ever went to the city anymore
Everything that they needed there was provided
By the flaming gypsies

WE DIDN'T HAVE HOUSES

We were repelled by the ones they put up

We were rich
We spread little stars on our bread

We were different
And we wrote down life in verse

IN FRONT OF THE CHURCH

Rain falls in our hair
While speaking with the priest
And the bony fingers of the mountain ashes
Massage our heads
Like the rosaries do our fingers

SAVING WORDS

I already wanted to finish the line with *clock*
When a deep voice uttered:
'SAVE THAT WORD!'
I wanted to start the next one with *dog*
When that same voice said
'SAVE THAT ONE TOO!'
I became seriously afraid

After midnight I sat down once again
I wrote, that *despair is just a decoration*
Once again I heard clearly:
'SAVE THAT WORD!'
I cried out in horror – which one then?
A deafening silence set in
My heart tumbled down
And suddenly was a scaredy-cat

The child in the next room wasn't sleeping, he had drilled
   a hole in the wall
He was regulating my work with an enormous horn

I SAW A CALM FISH

It wasn't swimming
It wasn't dead either
It was meditating

A COUPLE

They came here every day
Sat on a bench and read the paper
Trains flew by – back and forth
People stared at them through the window
Every day to and from work
The couple chose different times
So the audience would be bigger

THE SOUNDS PICKED UP BY THE PIANIST
DISSOLVE INTO FEELINGS AND PAST MEMORIES

The desire to seize the screen behind which he was hiding
    from the past, finally disappeared
It seemed, that he mercilessly pulled the music in his hands
    from the piano
And that he had at least twenty fingers
It totally slipped your mind, that there were also children,
    your husband and parents there
Together with the applause the wind threw open the window
    once again
And broke an enormous vase

WITH SEMICOLONS

I was lying down in the afternoon, then I got up, drank a cup
Of coffee and dove into your sun; hours minutes seconds later
I looked through the window and it seemed that the jasmine
Bushes were blossoming in July; that rippling is like a person
With poor vision, who has unwittingly invented impressionism;
I will dive in and the whole evening and night I will be in your
Sun like in a place before and after a made-up city where they
Both wait and forget the rain, the drops of which have yet to
Plan their birth in the cloud, which like Venus's kiss sliding
Past graze the mountain's summit where people also live

THE VIOLIN'S NECK FINISHED, THERE'S NO PLACE TO PUT THE BOW

I was able to make such a piercing sound
The glass shattered, everyone ran away

THE RESPONSE IS SILENCE

When she told her husband
There was another
He took his jacket from her shoulders
Put it on
And left
He loved the cinema
Because life doesn't happen like that

NO MOMENT FITS INSIDE ANOTHER

It seemed, it was all like yesterday
When in this place, looking at the window, I saw
Two women smoking something pretty good
I went there today and thought that they would be there
But no – the curtains were drawn
I thought perhaps it's not a real window
But further on there weren't curtains either
All the windows had been bricked up
I turned and went back, to where those curtains were
All the windows had been bricked up

Part Two

A POEM ABOUT TWO JURMALA TRAINS, HIDING AROUND OPPOSITE CORNERS AND WAITING TO SEE WHICH WILL APPEAR FIRST

They're like boys
Playing hide and go seek
For us on the platform we're sick of it already

A POEM ABOUT THE FACT THAT LIFE IS BETTER AT NIGHT THAN DURING THE DAY

I have to get up

A POEM ABOUT THE PHOTO OF A CHILD AT SUCH A YOUNG AGE THAT HE CAN'T HOLD HIS HEAD UP YET

You could see a grown-up's thumb hidden behind his back
Holding it up

A POEM ABOUT A WOMAN WALKING TOWARDS ME ON THE PAVEMENT WHO LOOKED INTO MY EYES

Two buttons
And I became shy

A POEM ABOUT HOW CHILDREN LIE TO THEIR PARENTS

We stood in the rain for a while
....
(All we did was drink a few glasses of lightning)

A POEM AS GRATITUDE FOR THE FACT THAT IN MY HEAD MY CHILDHOOD YARD IS THE SAME AS BEFORE

When I see the yard now with my own eyes
Which, like for everyone, are situated at the front part of
  the head
It gives the brain a signal, that the yard has become quite small
The brain doesn't believe it, goes home and sticks with its
  own opinion

A POEM ABOUT HOW HER BIRTHDAY HADN'T EVEN STARTED AND HOW AFTER FOUR AM WE COULDN'T FALL BACK ASLEEP

She said: 'The pain is raining on my head
Like liquid mercury on bare tree branches.'

A POEM ABOUT A MAN WHO WAS TOSSED OUT OF WORLD WAR TWO FOR DRINKING

He had a pain in his heart, he did
He died before he was thirty

A POEM ABOUT THE FACT THAT NO ONE HAD ANYTHING MORE TO SAY

Someone suggested we be silent
After some time I shut my eyes and… there was nothing there
My brain and an empty hallway alongside it
Neither stalactites, nor stalagmites
I hurriedly throw open my eyelids
A beautiful place where I await mornings

A POEM ABOUT THE FACT THAT I WENT BACK ALONG A LONG ROAD NEAR THAT JASMINE BUSH, WHICH GAVE OFF A PLEASANT SMELL, THE SAME AS IN MY CHILDHOOD, ALWAYS DURING THE SAME TIME OF YEAR OUTSIDE THE WINDOW OF MY ROOM

I had two heavy packages in my hands

A POEM ABOUT THE FACT THAT IT TOOK ME FOUR YEARS TO BUY A PUMP, WHICH CAN ALSO BE CALLED AN AIR PUMP, FOR PUMPING UP A BALL, WHAT HAPPENED WHEN I FINALLY DID, AND WHAT PROCEEDED AFTERWARDS

I would pump the ball up from time to time
But I never once played with it

A POEM ABOUT YOU GOING ALONG THE SEASHORE AND FORGETTING TO LOOK TOWARDS THE SEA

The sea is th-e-e-e-e-r-e
Like a gigantic fur coat

A POEM ABOUT HOW SHE CUT HER THROAT WITH A SCYTHE

It was the thinnest page of Sholokhov's thick
And Quiet Flows the Don

A POEM ABOUT THE FACT THAT IF WE, ARTISTS, BECOME FASCINATED WITH SOMETHING THEN IT'S FOR A LONG TIME

I kiss the sick
But I am not Jesus Christ
And I get sick as well

A POEM ABOUT HOW I SO WANTED MY OWN HOUSE, A DOG, A SMALL CAT AND A CHILD FROM YOU

A brief moment

A POEM ABOUT THE FACT THAT YOU HAVE TO DRUM UP THE COURAGE FOR ONCE

Organise your own wedding, live through it, wake up the
   next day and
Go where your eyes take you

A POEM ABOUT HOW SPRING PREVAILS OVER EVERYTHING ALIVE AND REVIVES THE DEAD

A white apple tree just laughs heartily
And strews its blossoms about
In a garden with forgotten musical instruments

A POEM ABOUT DOROTPOLE LAKE, INTO WHICH A GIRL IN A RED DRESS WADES

The landscape is completed

A POEM ABOUT HOW EACH CURVE OF YOURS
MATCHES EACH DIP OF MINE AND EACH
GROOVE OF MINE MATCHES EACH NOOK
OF YOURS THAT WE LIKE TO BREATHE EACH
OTHER IN AND THAT WE ARE TWO IN A PLACE
CONTAINING THE ENTIRE WORLD, INCLUDING
ASIA AND AFRICA

Man, it's a scary thought, but that's alright!

A POEM WHERE TWO GIRAFFES COME AND ONE BUTTS THE SUN IN SUCH A WAY THAT IT COMES CRASHING DOWN

Darkness

Part Three

BOUNDLESS

I like how your hair gallops
But in order for me to see it
I have to get to it

THE FRENCH LIEUTENANT'S WOMAN

Miss,
that sort of staring into the sea
Is very provocative

YOU CAN NEVER CRAWL OUT OF TWO HOLES AT THE SAME TIME

But I want to, and I go crazy
You unharness me totally, thank god
You kiss my temples and lie down to sleep
It would be horrible, if you weren't here
When I kick off the covers while sleeping
You tuck me in again with kisses

YOU WOULD CONTINUE TO COVER ME IN KISSES

And I wouldn't move
As the years passed
Stalactites and stalagmites would form

YOUR HEART IS AS JUICY AS A STRAWBERRY

But your skin – a sweet lettuce leaf
You lie in a meadow with lush greenery
And further on there's a raspberry bush, until the sun ceases
Your hair shines – blood vessels for a holy current
You are sweetness, wrapping itself in summer

WHEN YOU COME WITH A CAKE

We're not doing anything special, just becoming older
We don't clean the house, we don't go to any parties
We look at black and white photos from those times
When no one knew where we were for the entire day
And we went to someone's place and just believed they'd be
    at home
We receive kisses only from familiar lips
They are sensitive to departure
Then once again some sort of non-life-threatening illness
    appears like a road
You come to your senses on your birthday
Surfing the Internet
Without even having to take your clothes off

AND A CHILD BEGAN CRYING

My fellow travellers shut their mouths
They held beer bottles in their hands and forgot to drink
Both had travelled the long road of the migrant worker
From home, where abandoned children waited, left with
    their mothers
They knew they wouldn't hear that kind of crying after
    they left—
Their children will grow up
They won't see them every day
Both young guys became confused and grumbled, until the
    little one fell asleep
They didn't see the tears, because they tried to not look in
    that direction
The child cried in a strange way – like a violin

A MAN IN A LIGHT BROWN RAINCOAT

And a hat with rolled-up edges
Runs to the tram
His red tie tucked into a tie clip
The man is about seventy-five
And he has aged well
Strangely enough the man doesn't run to the first carriage
   in front
Which is closer
But to the last door of the second carriage – from experience,
   perhaps?
From the starting line he had a sprint of some sixty metres
Like in primary school during gym class in winter
He clearly has a hardiness
Which makes one think about powerful genes
The very best vitamins during the Soviet era
And membership in the KGB
Also about the fact that he isn't in those sacks [2]
But some special bag

---

2 A reference to sacks of KGB files containing possible information on
KGB agents and informants that were taken to Moscow after the collapse
of the USSR.

HOW FRIGHTENED A POET BECOMES, WHEN HE SUDDENLY SEES HIS WIFE'S FACE!

It is beautiful, but in a different way
For months all he recognises is her hand
Which puts a plate with food in front of him
All that time he is writing his long-form poem
Not taking into account, that poets get lost in their long-
    form poems
On Saturday (according to her, Saturday) evenings, a hand
    sets down a glass with wine
Then he leans back in his chair and squirms painfully
He grimaces like there's a razor in his shirt seams
He takes a few sips
Then coughing he throws himself back into his work
Until once again upon seeing that woman's face, he
    becomes frightened
Like a horse, which rears up on the side of the road from
    the cars

IT'S CRAZY, HOW MUCH WOMEN LIKE MY WHITE SHIRT!

I was stared at even by young women and, of course, not
    just young women
My wife didn't want to let me out of the house
And I had a feeling, that I could lose my virginity once again
Perhaps I needed to bring myself back down to earth and buy
    a greasy burger?
I would simply be a normal guy in a white shirt with a greasy
    burger – everyone does it!
However no, I need to be strong. I know men, who in this
    kind of situation
Stick their arms out to the side and soar boldly between
    aeroplanes
They are protected in the heavens
However they have to be conquered

IN SALZBURG

The centuries run up and down
On the stairs of the fortress
It provides sustenance for history
So it doesn't die without knowing its heirs
I am eating apple strudel in the valley
I'm drinking some water
Even last autumn is a hazy memory for me

REALITY IN THE MOUNTAINS

Women above the clouds are playing football
They have sandals on their naked feet and black skirts

One team's skirts have red diamond shapes and a green line
    along the bottom
The same as those in which they do all the house and field
    work

Here only broad beans, potatoes and a little wheat grow
You can get a little salt, flour and oil in the city for it

Day in and day out they eat potatoes

They don't train all that much
After work in the field there's not much time left over

It's just in the last few years their men allow their wives to
    play football
Because their wives are happier afterwards

The men are proud, if their wives beat other villages

It's a chance to get to the other side of the mountain and
    meet other women
If in the evening they want to get back, then they have to
    play right after a tough hike

The team's captain gives out coca leaves before the game
Then all of them are stronger, everyone has doping

They have no idea about football beyond the Andes of Peru
It doesn't even occur to them to wear shorts or boots

Those are moments, when they forget everything
People from the lower villages out of breath already after
    fifty metres up here
But they are able to run for miles

All the women enjoy themselves so much
That they feel so good together like the skin of one big
    happy woman

Nowhere so high up do women run after a ball
No one remembers, how it all started

THE REEDS ARE SWAYING ON THE EDGES OF THE MEDITERRANEAN

Now and then some break up into strips
One of them is already making the mouth of an oboe
   player ache

A FENCE SURROUNDING A FIELD

In the middle there's a pole with a sign on it that says:
    FOR SALE (telephone number)
Today the plot of land is being rented out to a dog training
    school
In the middle is a competent older lady, she's giving
    commands to the dogs and owners
The dogs aren't listening, they are all so huge and drag their
    owners along the ground
Along the fence like Roman chariots did with prisoners
The horrified passers-by cross to the other side of the street

AND HER HUSBAND DIED

It happened yesterday
In the night he had come to the door like he was alive
And shook the heart of this new widow
By morning he was gone, most likely forever
With closed eyelids like frozen ponds
And knowledge others can never recover
Brown leaves continue to fall outside the window
She lies there for another hour and thinks about
Why he didn't have any friends

DOWN

You can't run down the mountain anymore
It was simply running down a steep slope when you were a boy
No one can give that back to you
But no one owes you that
You could have run down the mountain more, so you
    wouldn't regret it now

OLD MAN

To eat an apple
Feel the taste
I can't bite it
I slice it with a knife
It's not the same

DELTA

An old woman shuffled toward the sea
Like a wrinkled river
She will lie in the sun for a while
Then with kids a century younger than her
Will hit a volley
Her spirit will spill out while serving

AN ENCOUNTER BETWEEN TWO MONKS IN THE MOUNTAINS

And instead of hello they say to one another affectionately:
'Remember death!'
Their flesh is an envelope, carrying a letter to the heavens

I LOST MY PRIEST'S PAPERS

They weren't necessary anymore anyway
The whirlwind was so fierce
That it blew away both the permit office
Where I was checked so thoroughly
And the cases with the wafers, which I frantically
Gripped with both hands—
Hundreds were waiting for them at a youth camp near Madrid
Like me they crouched down on the ground in panic
At the last moment it absorbed us like fresh slurry
Everything else was on the way up
Even the disciplined police on white horses
Even my priest's hat

GOD TAKES A WALK IN THE CITY PARK

And greets two grey-haired girlfriends on a park bench:
'I really would have changed your life, if there hadn't been those
  beliefs, those traditions
You could love someone in your heart as much as you wanted
Cut your hair short, put on sunglasses and go into society
That wasn't the main thing anyway – you had eyes, ears, hands,
  legs.'
They sit down somewhere else, but you can't just put your life
  down somewhere else anymore
Life isn't just a ray of sunshine, like the ones bothering them at
  that moment

Phenomena

Eduards Aivars

Translated from Latvian by Jayde Will

Supported by the Ministry of Culture for the Republic of
Latvia and the Latvian Writers' Union

Kultūras ministrija

Latvijas Rakstnieku savienība **Latvija 100**

CYNGOR LLYFRAU CYMRU
WELSH BOOKS COUNCIL

Parthian, Cardigan SA43 1ED
www.parthianbooks.com
First published in 2018
© Eduards Aivars 2018
© Translation Jayde Will 2018
ISBN 9781912109098
Design and layout by Alison Evans
Printed by Pulsio